Contents

WHAT IS SOUND?

Sound is a type of energy that travels in waves of vibrations.

Noises that we hear are made by things vibrating. When something is vibrating, it is moving backwards and forwards a tiny amount, really fast. Normally these vibrations are so small and fast we can't see them, but we can sometimes feel them.

Good vibrations

An easy way to feel sound **vibrations** is to put your fingers on your throat, and go "Ahhhh"! Air from your lungs passes through your voice box. Your voice box contains two soft flaps called **vocal chords**. The air rushing past them makes them vibrate very fast, from 100 to 1000 times per second.

Ahhhhhh!

What's all the buzz about?

Why do things start vibrating and making sounds in the first place? It can happen in lots of ways, for example when an object is hit, or when two objects are rubbed against each other. Sound is often made by air rushing past something, or through a hollow object. This is how wind instruments make a noise.

Toooooot!

Ba-Ba-BOOM

The strongest vibrations make the loudest sounds. Have you ever sat near a road and felt your whole body move when a big, noisy truck goes past? This is caused by the powerful vibrations from the truck travelling through the ground and the air and vibrating your body.

TRUE or FALSE?

Sound vibrations can cause delicate objects like wine glasses to break apart – true or false?

Answer on page 28

Sound on the MOVE

Sound waves need 'matter' in order to travel.

When objects vibrate, they jiggle the air around them. Although air looks empty, it is actually made of tiny bits called **molecules**. The sound travels as the vibrations are passed along in waves from one air molecule to the next.

Heave!

Imagine a queue of people standing close together, holding the person in front. The person at the back gives a hard push into the person in front of them, who can't help but push into the person in front of *them*. The push travels along the queue, like a wave. But the person at the back bounces back slightly after giving the hard push. This pulls the person in front of them back again, and so on.

What's the speed of sound?

There is no such thing as one 'speed of sound'. Sound travels at different speeds through different substances, but it travels through air at around 1,230 kmph.

6

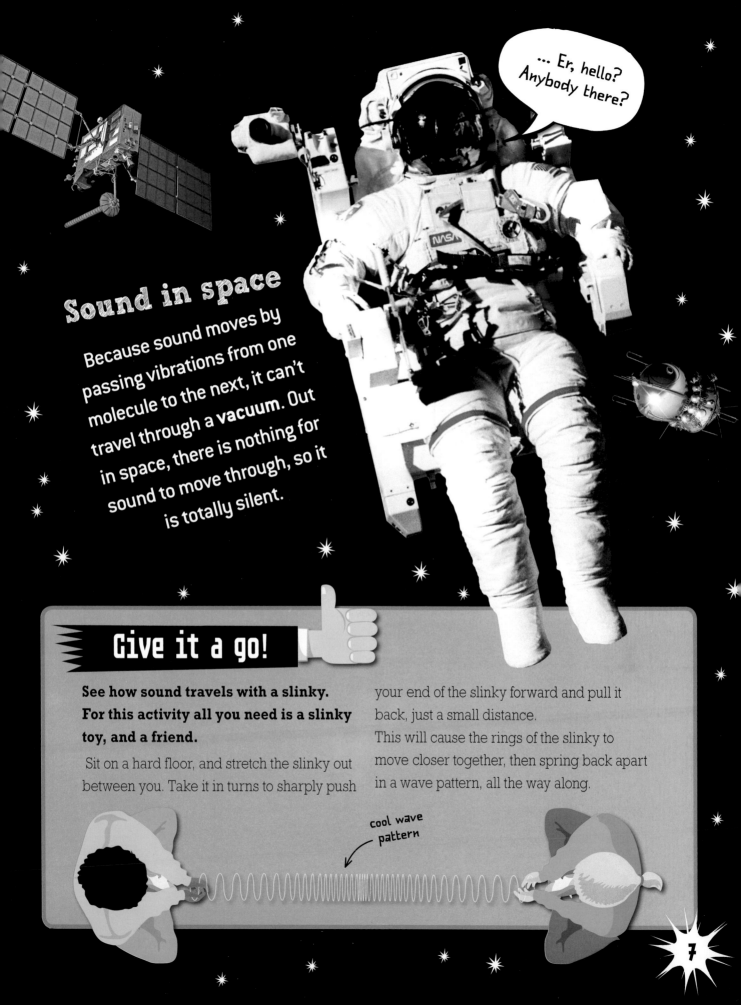

... Er, hello? Anybody there?

Sound in space

Because sound moves by passing vibrations from one molecule to the next, it can't travel through a **vacuum**. Out in space, there is nothing for sound to move through, so it is totally silent.

Give it a go!

See how sound travels with a slinky. For this activity all you need is a slinky toy, and a friend.

Sit on a hard floor, and stretch the slinky out between you. Take it in turns to sharply push your end of the slinky forward and pull it back, just a small distance.

This will cause the rings of the slinky to move closer together, then spring back apart in a wave pattern, all the way along.

cool wave pattern

LOUD and *soft*

The volume of a sound depends on how much energy is used to make it.

The **volume** of a sound is how loud or soft it is. Louder sounds carry more energy – that's why shouting is more tiring than whispering. Sounds also get quieter the further away they are. This is because sound waves lose energy as they travel over long distances.

Decibel scale

The volume of a sound is measured in **decibels**. 0 decibels is total silence, while sounds louder than 130 decibels can damage your ears.

The decibel scale doesn't go up in equal amounts like a ruler, though. 20 decibels is not twice as loud as 10 decibels, it is ten times as loud. And 30 decibels is ten times as loud as 20 decibels. So a 60 decibel sound is a million times louder than a 10 decibel sound!

NORMAL
TALKING
50
DECIBELS

AMBULANCE
SIREN
120
DECIBELS

DOG
BARKING
100
DECIBELS

BIRD CALL
40
DECIBELS

RUSTLING LEAVES
20
DECIBELS

AIRCRAFT OVERHEAD
90
DECIBELS

Riddle me this!

Sounds are less clear on a windy day. Why is this?

Answer on page 28

Can you hear me now?

Give it a go!

With a friend, try a simple experiment to see how sound gets weaker as it travels.

Go outside into a field or playground. Standing close to each other, speak at a normal volume. You should be able to hear each other easily.

Now try moving a few meters back, and speaking at the same volume. How far apart do you have to stand before you can't hear what each other are saying?

HIGH AND LOW

Fast vibrations make high-pitched noises, slow vibrations make low-pitched noises.

What's the difference between the tweet of a bird, and the roar of a lion? Apart from the fact one would be a lot scarier if you heard it behind you, a bird's tweet is a high-pitched sound, and a roar is a low-pitched sound. The **pitch** of a sound depends on how fast the vibrations happen.

What is frequency?

The pitch of a sound depends on its **frequency**. This means how many sound waves are made in a certain time, or how fast the vibrations are happening.

When an object vibrates, it pushes out a certain number of sound waves per second. The more sound waves per second, the higher the frequency, and the higher-pitched the noise is.

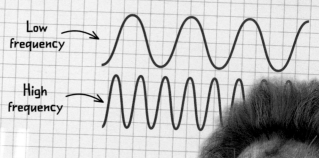

Low frequency

High frequency

You can see the effect of frequency in action by twanging a ruler on the edge of a table.

When only a <u>short</u> part of the ruler is twanged, the end vibrates much faster, and makes a high-pitched sound.

When a <u>long</u> part of the ruler is twanged you can see that the end vibrates slowly, and a low sound is made.

That hertz!

Frequency is measured in **hertz** (Hz). Humans can hear sounds between 20 Hz and 20,000 Hz. Sounds that are too low for us to hear are called **infrasounds**, and sounds too high to hear are called **ultrasounds**. Dolphins can hear the highest frequencies, up to 280,000 Hz! Read more about infrasound and ultrasound on pages 18 and 19.

Mighty mice

Squeak! Mice use noises outside of the range of predators' hearing. This lets them communicate secretly, without being noticed!

Sound and hearing

Our ears sense sound waves, which our brains translate into the sounds we hear.

In order to hear the sounds that surround us, we need ears. Our ears are made up of very sensitive little parts that jiggle when sound waves hit them. Nerves then send messages to the brain, which translates them into the sounds we hear.

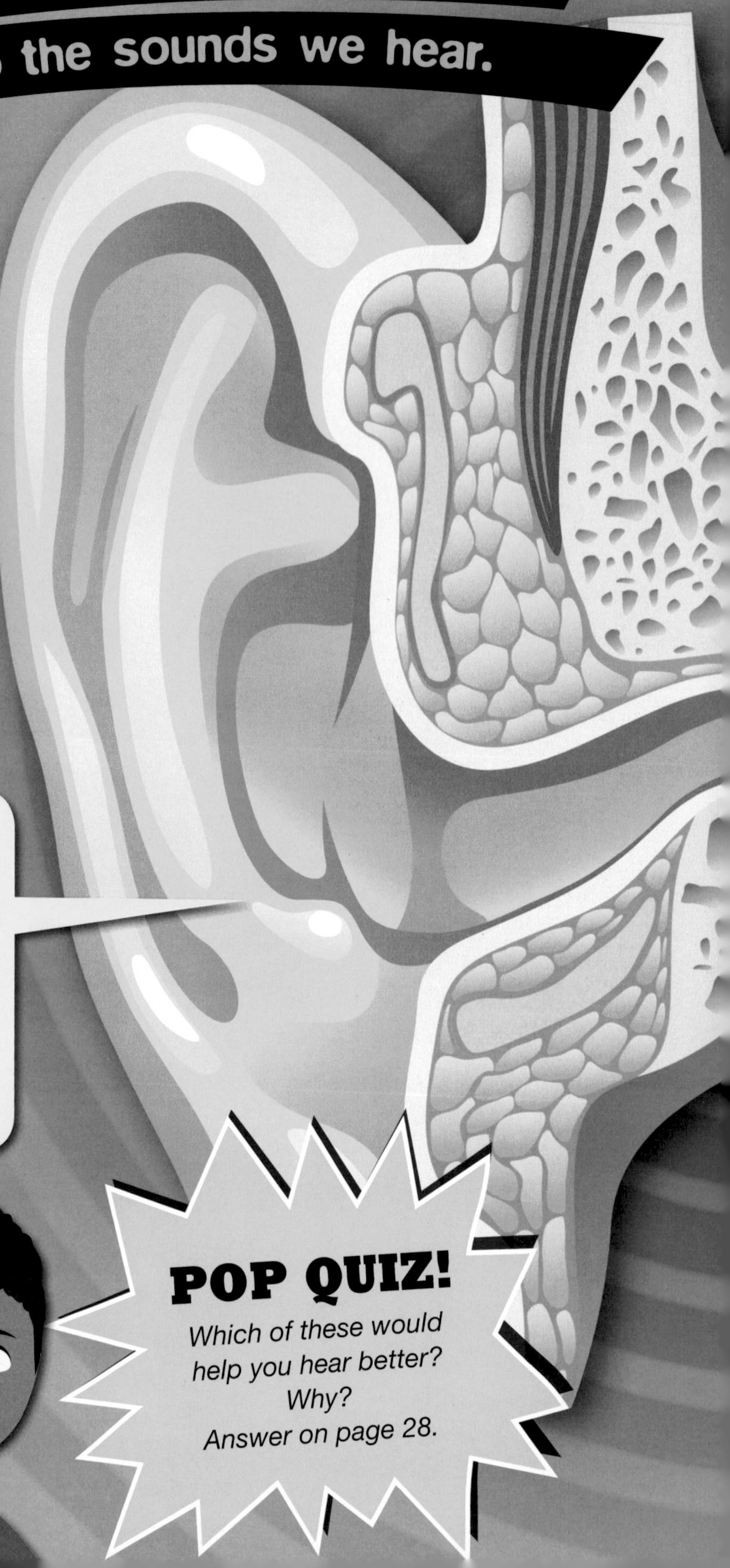

1

The **pinna** is the flappy bit on the outside of your head. It acts like a funnel, catching sound waves, and sending them down your ear canal to the ear drum.

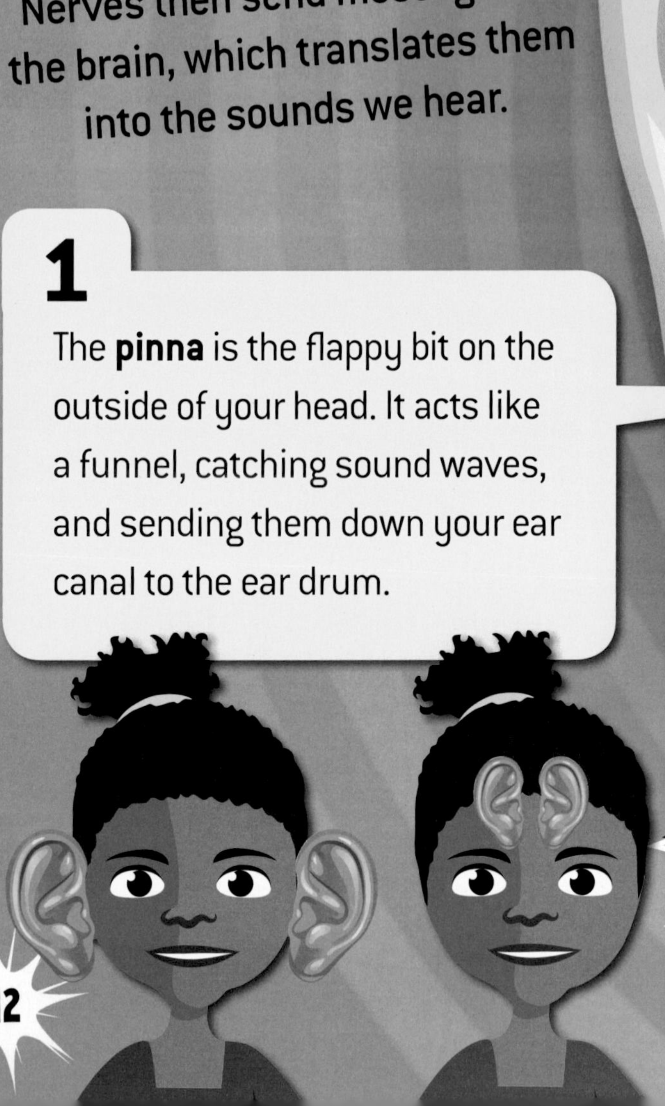

POP QUIZ!

Which of these would help you hear better? Why?
Answer on page 28.

12

2

The **eardrum** is a thin layer of skin, like a musical drum. Sound waves hit the ear drum, which is attached to three small bones called **ossicles**.

Give it a go!

Can you listen to sounds... without your ears?

Try this: turn on a sound source that has a single speaker, like a radio. Block your ears with ear plugs, and turn the music down until you can't hear it. Hold a toothbrush between your teeth at the handle end. Touch the brush end to the radio speaker. Can you hear it now?

3

The ossicles pass the vibrations along to the **cochlear**, which is a spiral-shaped tube filled with liquid and tiny hairs. The vibrations move through the liquid, making the hairs vibrate.

4

Nerves touching the tiny hairs in the cochlear send the information to the brain as electrical signals. The brain understands these electrical signals as sounds.

What is an echo?

An echo is a repeated sound, made when sound waves bounce back.

Have you ever stood in a tunnel and shouted 'hello!', and heard a quiet 'hello-oo-oo...' come back? This is because just like light, sound can be reflected. When sound is reflected, it makes a kind of 'ghost' of the original sound, which we call an **echo**.

Most echoes are too weak for us to hear, but in places with lots of hard surfaces like a tunnel or a cave, we can hear the reflected sound as echoes.

What makes echoes?

Although sound can travel easily through solids, liquids and gases, moving between substances is more difficult. When sound travels through air and hits a solid surface, not all the sound energy carries on. Instead, some of the sound energy bounces back, like a rubber ball.

Some sound bounces back (this is the echo)

Some sound is absorbed by the rock

Useful echoes

Echolocation is a way of 'seeing' the world using sound, by using echoes to sense where objects or surfaces are. Animals such as bats, dolphins and whales send out sound waves, which bounce off objects and other creatures nearby. Bats can tell the size and location of their tiny insect prey by the echoes that come back, allowing them to hunt in the dark.

Did you know?

Bats' echolocation is so accurate they can sense objects the size of a human hair!

Super sonar

Humans use echolocation too — although we need technology to do it! **Sonar** stands for 'sonic navigation and ranging', and is used for all sorts of reasons.

The navy use sonar to identify and locate submarines and other ships. It can be used by fishermen to find schools of fish, or in exploration to map the seabed, measure depth, or find submerged shipwrecks.

Blocking sound

Some materials absorb sound waves and block sound.

Car alarms blaring, lawn mowers roaring, music playing when you want to sleep ... some sounds are very annoying, but blocking them out can be a tricky business.

Unlike light, sound can easily travel through solids, liquids and gases. However, we can use our understanding of how sound waves travel to figure out ways to block sound.

Thick wall

Air gap

Soundproofing buildings

We know that passing from one substance to another causes sound waves to be partly reflected, so one technique to block sound inside buildings is to build thick walls with large air gaps inside.

Brrmmm!
Brrmmm!

Ah, peace and quiet!

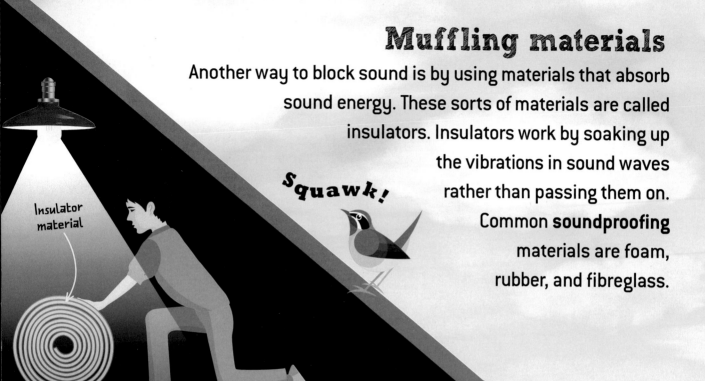

Muffling materials

Another way to block sound is by using materials that absorb sound energy. These sorts of materials are called insulators. Insulators work by soaking up the vibrations in sound waves rather than passing them on. Common **soundproofing** materials are foam, rubber, and fibreglass.

Insulator material

Squawk!

Give it a go!

Try this activity with a friend, or use a small speaker (like a mobile phone) to find out which materials are the best insulators.

You will need a cardboard tube (such as an empty kitchen roll), and a selection of materials to test, such as bubble-wrap, fabric, kitchen towel, or anything else you can think of.

Start by putting the empty tube to your ear, and having your friend speak into it (not too loudly), or playing sound from a phone.

Next, test the different materials one by one by stuffing them into the tube, and having your friend speak, or play the sound again.

Always keep the volume the same. Which material blocks the most sound? Which blocks the least?

ULTRASOUND AND INFRASOUND

Sound that is too high or too low for us to hear is called ultrasound and infrasound.

Our ears have evolved to only detect sound that has a pitch (or frequency) roughly near the pitch of a human voice. Much higher and lower sounds exist, but we can't naturally hear them. Very high sounds are called ultrasound. Very low-pitched sounds are called infrasound.

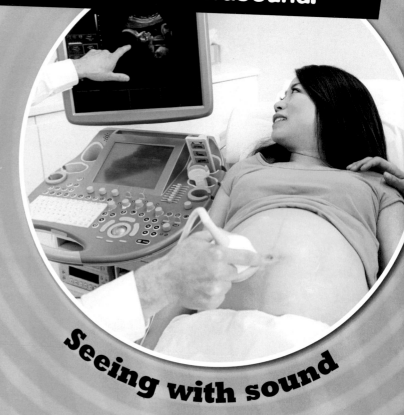

Seeing with sound

Although we can't hear it, ultrasound is very useful. The sound waves are very fast, and reflect better than lower sound waves. It is used for underwater echolocation (sonar), but has medical uses too. Read more about this on page 15.

POP QUIZ!

Can you guess which of these is a real use for ultrasound? Answer on page 28.

1 Demolishing buildings

2 Cleaning glasses

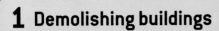

Infrasound

Very low sounds, called infrasounds, are given off by natural events such as earthquakes, volcanoes and avalanches, as well as by severe weather events like hurricanes. Scientists can use infrasounds to monitor or detect these events before they happen, or to pinpoint their locations.

Spooky sounds

Infrasound has been suggested as a possible explanation for ghost sightings! Although they can't hear it, some people exposed to infrasound get feelings of nervousness and sadness, and other odd sensations that might be mistaken for a paranormal experience.

Did you know?

Infrasound can travel over large distances without running out of energy, and some animals make use of this. Elephants have been discovered to communicate with infrasound up to 10 kilometres away!

19

ANIMAL HEARING

Animals make and use sounds in lots of different ways.

Just like humans, animals use noises to communicate, sending out messages warning each other of danger, or calling out to attract a mate. Animals also use sound and hearing to find and hunt for food.

HOPE SHE'S GOT MY CRUNCHIES ...

AMAZING SENSES

Have you ever seen a pet dog or cat perk up at the sound of their owner coming home, well before you could hear anyone coming? Compared to humans, many animals have incredible hearing. This is because, in the wild, animals rely on good hearing to find and catch their food — or to avoid being eaten!

AHEM, I HEARD THAT!

DOG DETECTOR

Humans can hear sounds up to 20,000 hz, but dogs can hear sounds up to 40,000 hz. This allows dog trainers to use whistles that are silent to us, but dogs can hear clearly. Dogs can also hear sounds from about four times as far away as humans.

COOL CATS

Cats have even better hearing than dogs, sensing sounds up to 60,000 hz. They have 30 different muscles that allow them to move their ears around independently and in all directions, so they can pinpoint exactly where a sound is coming from.

I CAN HEAR YOU ... I'M JUST IGNORING YOU.

OK, PUT YOUR FINS UP

STUNNING SHRIMP

The tiny pistol shrimp is only the size of your finger, but it's one of the loudest animals on earth! It has a large claw that it can click at such high speed, it causes a bubble of pressure to shoot out like a bullet, stunning its prey. The sound can reach 218 decibels, louder than a gunshot.

Riddle me this!

What do a barn owl and a satellite dish have in common?

Answer on page 29.

21

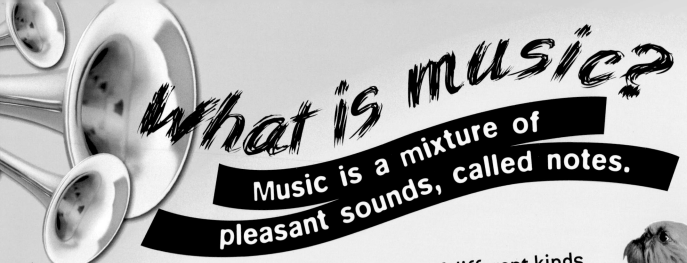

what is music?

Music is a mixture of pleasant sounds, called notes.

Pop, rock, classical, jazz ... there are lots of different kinds of music, but they are all made up of **notes**. Notes are the sounds made by musical instruments, and each note has a different pitch. By combining notes at different speeds and rhythms, we create songs or tunes that are nice to listen to.

Wind instruments are blown to vibrate air inside pipes.

String instruments have strings which vibrate when plucked or **bowed**.

Bash, Blow, Pluck!

Musical instruments make **notes** in different ways.

Let's jam fellas!

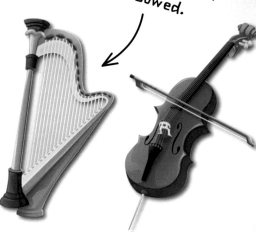

Percussion instruments make sounds when they are hit or struck.

EYE SPY!

How many musical instruments can you count?

Make music by creating your own simple string instrument.

Find an empty tissue box or plastic tub (such as a margarine tub), and a handful of elastic bands of different sizes and thicknesses.

Stretch the elastic bands around the box and pluck them with your fingers to play.

Try making the elastic bands shorter and tighter by tying knots in them. Do they make different notes? What do you notice about the vibrations?

elastic bands

How it works

strings

All string instruments, including your elastic band guitar, work basically the same way. The strings vibrate when plucked – but a string vibrating by itself isn't very loud.

So all string instruments have some kind of hollow sound box that **amplifies** the noise. In your elastic band guitar, it's the tissue box.

The vibration from the strings travel into the sound box. The sound box is bigger than the string and so sends out soundwaves through the air to our ears more powerfully.

Twang!

sound box

RECORDING SOUNDS

Sound recordings reproduce the vibrations that made the original sound.

The technology to record and reproduce sound is a very important part of everyday life. Without it, we couldn't watch television, listen to music or radio, or talk on the telephone. The first sound recording and reproduction was made by Thomas Edison in 1877.

The phonograph

Thomas Edison developed an invention called the **phonograph** in 1877. Speaking into a sound box caused a needle to vibrate, and scratch a pattern onto tinfoil wrapped around a cardboard cylinder. To replay the sound, a second needle was run back over the scratches, faintly reproducing the original vibrations.

OMG I LOVE this song!

AUDIO RECORDING TECHNOLOGY TIMELINE

The first records in the 1880s were made on wax cylinders.

Discs made from an insect-produced resin called shellac were popular in the early 20th century. Shellac was later replaced by a type of plastic called vinyl.

Magnetic tapes were invented in Germany during the Second World War, but they didn't become really popular until the 1970s and 80s.

Vibrations in, vibrations out

To record sound, microphones pick up the vibrations and translate them into electrical signals, which are stored or transmitted. At the other end, speakers turn the electrical signals back into vibrations that make the sounds.

microphone

Spot the sound

How many things can you see in this picture that record or reproduce sound?

The first music compact discs (CDs) were sold in the 1980s. CDs were a digital way of storing music, read by lasers.

Most people now listen to music through computers and phones, listening to downloaded MP3s, or streaming from the internet.

SOUND and SCIENCE

Scientists are working with sound

in amazing new ways.

We already use sound waves in all sorts of important technology, from medical ultrasound scans to exploring the depths of the ocean. But scientists are developing more and more cutting-edge ways to use sound.

Real life 'tractor beams'

The idea of a 'tractor beam' that can push and pull floating objects around is something straight out of science fiction. But scientists have developed a sonic tractor beam that can levitate and move objects in thin air.

Levitating object

Speakers emit high-intensity sound waves

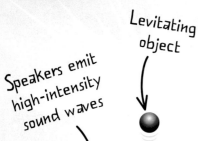

Sonic surgery

The sonic tractor beams can only move small objects, but they could be used to do surgery inside a patient's body without having to make any cuts from the outside.

Bionic hearing

Cochlear implants have been helping deaf people hear, by connecting a microphone on the outside of the head to the nerve that sends signals from the ear to the brain.

New cochlear implant technology is being developed that goes a step further, using the natural outer ear as a microphone, and inserting a tiny chip straight into the middle ear. The chip would be charged wirelessly through a smart phone while the user talked on the phone!

microphone

If I fart in here, there's no covering up.

Extreme silence

Scientists in Minneapolis in the US have created a room that blocks 99.99% of sound, and holds the Guinness World Record for the world's quietest place. Being inside the 'anechoic chamber' for even just 15 minutes can cause hallucinations, and people report being able to hear the sounds of their own internal organs!

27

And the answer is...

Page 5

True or false: TRUE. All objects have something called 'natural resonance'. This is a particular speed they vibrate at. By playing loud sounds of the same vibration speed next to the object, it can cause the object to vibrate so hard, it breaks apart!

Page 9

Riddle me this: Sounds are less clear on a windy day because sound needs air molecules to travel. Wind moves air around, affecting the movement of the sound waves.

Page 12

Pop quiz: Bigger ears would help you hear better, as they would capture more sound waves. Cupping your ear with your hand has the same effect. Having ears on the side of our head helps us in point where a sound is coming from. Having our ears close together on the front of our heads would make this more difficult.

Page 18

Pop quiz: Ultrasound is used for cleaning delicate items like jewellery or glasses. The objects are put into water, then ultrasound vibrations cause tiny bubbles to form, which dislodge bits of dirt. Although very, very loud sounds can damage buildings, it is only lower frequency sounds that have this effect, and only at very loud volumes.

Page 21

Riddle me this: Barn owls have very unique faces. Shaped like a disc, they funnel sounds waves in a similar way to a satellite dish. This gives them incredible hearing, so they can locate and capture prey in total darkness.

Page 22

Eye spy! There are 13 instruments hidden on the page.

Page 25

Spot the sound: There are six objects that record or reproduce sound: earphones, telephone, television, laptop, smart phone, radio.

Glossary

Amplify Make louder

Bowed (instrument) A string instrument, such as a violin, that is played by rubbing a bow of cord or hair across the strings

Cochlear A spiral-shaped part of the inner ear filled with fluid

Decibel A unit for measuring the loudness of sound

Eardrum A thin piece of skin in the middle ear that collects vibrations

Echo A repeated sound made when sound energy bounces back off a surface

Echolocation A way of sensing objects by bouncing sound waves off them

Energy Power to move or do work

Frequency How quickly the vibrations in a sound wave are made

Hertz A unit for measuring frequency and pitch of sounds

Infrasound Sounds too low for humans to hear

Molecules The smallest pieces a substance is made of, too small to be seen by the naked eye

Nerves Fibres that send messages around the body

Notes Sounds with different pitches made by musical instruments

Ossicles Tiny bones in the middle ear

Phonograph The first invention that could record and replay sound

Pinna The outer, visible part of the ear

Pitch How high or low a sound is

Sonar Technology that uses sound to detect the location and movement of objects underwater

Soundproofing Using materials to stop sound getting through

Ultrasound Sound too high for humans to hear

Vacuum Completely empty space without anything in it (even air)

Vibrations Tiny backwards and forwards movements

Vocal chords Flaps of muscle in the throat that vibrate to make sound when air passes through

Volume The loudness of a sound

Further reading

Disgusting and Dreadful Science:
Ear-Splitting Sounds and Other Vile Noises
Anna Claybourne (Franklin Watts, 2013)

Project Science: Sound
Sally Hewitt (Franklin Watts, 2014)

How Does Science Work: Sound
Carol Ballard (Wayland, 2014)

Mind Webs: Light and Sound
Anna Claybourne (Wayland, 2014)

Moving up with Science: Sound
Peter Riley (Watts, 2015)

Websites

www.explainthatstuff.com/sound
An easy-to-understand introduction to sound, and how it behaves.

www.ducksters.com/science/sound101
Facts about sound, with experiments to try.

www.bbc.co.uk/education/topics/zgffr82/resources/1
Lots of video clips all about sound.

www.exploratorium.edu/snacks/subject/sound
Fun projects and activities exploring sound and vibrations.

Index